International Cooking Collection

Summer Desserts

International
Cooking Collection

Summer Desserts
Carole Handslip

CONTENTS

Published exclusively for Cupress (Canada) Ltd
20 Torbay Road, Markham, Ontario L3R 1G6 Canada
by Woodhead-Faulkner (Publishers) Ltd, Simon & Schuster International Group

This edition first published 1988
© Woodhead-Faulkner (Publishers) Ltd 1988
All rights reserved
ISBN 0–920691–54–4
Printed and bound in Italy

INTRODUCTION

Whether you want to make the simplest fruit salad or an exotic strawberry extravaganza, here you will find plenty of exciting, original and attractive ideas.

Although I have included some elaborate desserts, my own favorites are the simple mixtures of those delicious fresh fruits which are available in such vast variety during the summer months—raspberries, redcurrants and strawberries, to name but a few. Adding a little liqueur to any fresh fruit dish transforms it into something special. For an attractive finishing touch, use soft fruit leaves and scented herbs to decorate.

Ice creams and sorbets are also very much in demand during the summer. These, too, are easy to prepare, and home-made ones are far superior to the commercial varieties. Any fruit puree, many of the fragrant herb teas and even elderflowers can make wonderful ice creams and sorbets. A fresh, sharp fruit puree can also be turned into a tangy fruit fool or a creamy mousse in minutes.

I nearly always try to prepare desserts in advance and leave them in the refrigerator until required, so that a minimum of last-minute attention is involved. However, there is one chapter devoted to hot desserts, and obviously some of these do need to be made at the last minute. They would probably be more suitable to serve to the family, rather than when entertaining.

A well-chosen dessert can make or break a meal. It is important to choose a dessert that complements the main course. After a rich main course, choose a light, slightly sharp fruit dish or a sorbet. To round off a lighter meal, opt for a gateau or pastry dessert.

You will find recipes appropriate for all occasions in the following pages—and don't hide this book away during the winter! Summer fruits freeze well and most of these desserts can be made out of season, using frozen fruit.

NOTES

All spoon measurements are level.

Ovens should be preheated to the temperature specified.

Use U.S. grade large eggs unless otherwise stated.

Sauce recipes are marked with an asterisk and given in the reference section (pages 78–9). Increase or decrease the basic quantities in proportion to obtain the amount required.

FRUIT DESSERTS

PEARS WITH CASSIS

A popular dessert in France, where creme de cassis
originates. You can poach the pears lightly if you prefer,
but I like to use juicy dessert pears and serve them as
they are.

3 cups blueberries	*2 tablespoons creme de*
¹/₄ cup superfine sugar	*cassis (optional)*
¹/₂ cup water	*6 dessert pears*

Serves 6
Preparation time:
20 minutes
Cooking time:
10 minutes
Freezing:
Recommended for
sauce only

1. Place the blueberries, sugar and water in a pan and
cook gently for about 10 minutes, stirring occasionally,
until soft.
2. Puree in a food processor or blender, then sieve to
remove the seeds. Leave to cool, then add the creme de
cassis, if using.
3. Peel, halve and core the pears; arrange on individual
dishes. Spoon over the sauce and serve immediately.

SUMMER FRUIT COMPOTE

2 cups mixed blueberries	*2 cups quartered*
and redcurrants	*strawberries*
2 tablespoons honey	*2 tablespoons Grand*
¹/₄ cup orange juice	*Marnier*
1 teaspoon arrowroot	

Serves 4
Preparation time:
15 minutes, plus
cooling
Cooking time:
10 minutes
Freezing:
Not recommended

1. Place the blueberries and redcurrants, honey and
orange juice in a pan, bring to the boil, then cover and
simmer gently for 10 minutes until softened.
2. Strain the fruit and place in a bowl. Return the syrup to
the pan.
3. Blend the arrowroot with a little water until smooth,
then stir into the syrup. Bring to the boil, stirring constantly until thickened and clear.
4. Pour over the berries and currants, add the strawberries and Grand Marnier, mix together gently and leave
to cool.
5. Turn into a glass serving bowl and chill until required.
Serve with Cremets*, yogurt or cream.

CHERRIES WITH ORANGE

12 oz can sour cherries
2 teaspoons arrowroot
grated rind and juice of
    1 orange
3 tablespoons kirsch
6 tablespoons heavy cream

1 egg white
1 tablespoon honey
about 40 amaretti biscuits
orange rind shreds (see
    below) to decorate

Serves 4
Preparation time:
30 minutes
Freezing:
Not recommended

1. Drain the cherries, place the juice in a pan and bring to the boil. Blend the arrowroot with the orange juice; add to the syrup, stirring constantly until thickened.
2. Pit the cherries, then add to the syrup with 2 tablespoons of the kirsch. Leave to cool.
3. Meanwhile, mix the remaining kirsch with the orange rind, add to the cream and whip until soft peaks form.
4. Beat the egg white until stiff, then beat in the honey. Fold into the orange cream.
5. Break each amaretti biscuit into 2 or 3 pieces and arrange in 4 individual glass bowls in alternate layers with the cream and cherries, finishing with a layer of cream.
6. Decorate with orange rind shreds and chill until required.

Orange or lemon rind shreds: Pare the rind thinly, using a potato peeler. Cut into very fine strips, about 1½ inches long. Blanch in boiling water for 2 minutes. Drain, rinse in cold water, drain again and pat dry with a paper towel. Use to decorate desserts.

PINEAPPLE SNOW

1 small pineapple
2 tablespoons kirsch
2 egg whites

2 tablespoons honey
frosted leaves (see page 42)
    to decorate

Serves 4–6
Preparation time:
15 minutes
Freezing:
Not recommended

1. Halve the pineapple lengthways, remove the hard central core and scoop out the flesh. Place in a food processor or blender with the kirsch and work until smooth.
2. Beat the egg whites until stiff, then beat in the honey.
3. Fold in the pineapple puree, spoon into wine glasses and decorate with frosted leaves. Serve immediately, as the dessert separates on standing.

PEACHES CARDINALE

One of the quickest and most refreshing summer desserts. For an equally pleasant change, use Strawberry Sauce* instead of Melba Sauce.

*²/₃ cup Melba Sauce**
1 tablespoon framboise liqueur or kirsch

4 peaches
2 tablespoons slivered almonds, toasted

1. Mix together the melba sauce and liqueur.
2. Dip the peaches in boiling water for about 8 seconds, then remove the skins. Cut in half, remove the pits and arrange on 4 individual plates.
3. Spoon over the sauce and sprinkle with the almonds.

Serves 4
Preparation time:
10 minutes, plus making sauce
Freezing:
Not recommended

TROPICAL FRUIT MOLD

This delicious dessert can be made with any fruits, but banana and guava do give it the tropical touch.

1¹/₄ cups tropical fruit juice   *2 bananas, sliced*
1 envelope gelatin   *2 pears, peeled, quartered,*
14 oz can guavas in syrup   *cored and sliced*

Serves 4–6
Preparation time:
15 minutes, plus
setting time
Freezing:
Not recommended

1. Place ¼ cup of the tropical fruit juice in a small pan, sprinkle over the gelatin and leave to soak for 5 minutes. Heat gently until dissolved, then mix with the remaining juice in a bowl.
2. Drain the guavas and add the syrup to the bowl. Slice the guavas and add to the bowl with the bananas and pears.
3. Pour into 4 or 6 individual molds, depending on their size; alternatively pour into a 4 cup mold. Chill for 2 hours, to set.
4. To turn out, dip the mold quickly into hot water and invert onto a serving plate.

ICED MANGO SOUP

A delightful way to finish off a sunny summer lunch in the garden. Simple to make, so you don't have to spend too long in the kitchen away from the sun!

2 mangoes   *¹/₄ cup sour or heavy cream*
²/₃ cup orange juice   *a little milk (optional)*
²/₃ cup sweet white wine

Serves 4
Preparation time:
10 minutes
Freezing:
Recommended

1. Cut the mangoes either side of the pit and scoop out all the flesh. Place in a food processor or blender with the orange juice and work until smooth.
2. Stir in the wine, then pour into individual soup bowls and chill until required.
3. Thin the cream with a little milk if necessary, then swirl a spoonful into the center of each bowl.

STRAWBERRY CHARTREUSE

A very simple dessert to make, and one that looks magnificent when cut. It also looks good sliced onto individual plates and surrounded with the sauce

1 mango
1 kiwi fruit, peeled and
  sliced
1 cup strawberries, halved
1 dessert pear, peeled and
  chopped

1¼ cups orange juice
1 envelope gelatin
2 tablespoons Grand
  Marnier
⅔ cup Strawberry Sauce*

Serves 6
Preparation time:
30 minutes, plus
making sauce and
setting time
Freezing:
Not recommended

1. Cut the mango either side of the pit. Scoop out and chop all the flesh. Place in a 4 cup ring mold or 7½ × 3½ × 2½ inch loaf pan with the kiwi fruit, strawberries and pear.
2. Place ⅔ cup of the orange juice in a small pan and sprinkle over the gelatin. Leave to soak for 5 minutes, then heat very gently until dissolved.
3. Add the remaining orange juice and the Grand Marnier, pour into the mold or pan and chill for 2 hours, until set.
4. To turn out, dip the mold or pan quickly into hot water, then invert onto a serving plate. Cut into slices, and serve with the strawberry sauce.

CHOCOLATE ORANGE CUPS

7 oz baker's semi-sweet
   chocolate, broken into
   pieces
4 oranges

2 tablespoons Grand
   Marnier
1 cup heavy cream

1. Place the chocolate in a small bowl over a pan of hot water. Bring the water to the boil, then turn off the heat and leave until the chocolate has melted; be careful not to allow any water to get into the bowl. Leave to cool.
2. Spread 2 tablespoons of the chocolate onto waxed paper and leave until just set. Cut into squares and then into triangles, using a ruler and sharp knife; set aside.
3. Spoon half of the remaining chocolate into 8 paper cake cases and, using the handle of a teaspoon, spread it over the inside of each case. Leave for about 1 hour to set at room temperature, then cover with a second coat of chocolate. Leave to set.
4. Finely grate the zest of 1 orange, mix with the Grand Marnier; stir into the cream. Whip until it holds its shape.
5. Remove the paper from the chocolate cases and pipe orange cream into each case. Top with chocolate triangles.
6. Peel the remaining oranges; divide all the oranges into segments, discarding all pith. Arrange the chocolate cups and orange segments on individual plates to serve.

Serves 8
Preparation time:
35 minutes, plus
setting time
Freezing:
Not recommended

STRAWBERRY ROMANOFF

This light, creamy dessert is perfect for warm summer
days. It is best served with crisp cookies.

⅔ cup heavy cream
*2 tablespoons Grand
    Marnier*
1 egg white
1 tablespoon honey

⅔ cup sour cream
3 cups strawberries, halved
*4 frosted strawberry leaves
    (see page 42) to decorate*

Serves 4
Preparation time:
20 minutes
Freezing:
Not recommended

1. Combine the heavy cream and Grand Marnier, then
whip until it holds its shape.
2. Beat the egg white until stiff, then beat in the honey.
Fold into the cream with the sour cream.
3. Set aside a few strawberry halves for decoration. Fold
the rest into the cream mixture.
4. Spoon into 4 glass serving dishes and chill until
required. Decorate with the reserved strawberries and the
frosted leaves.

SPICED APPLE LAYER

Choose tall glasses so that the layers in this delicious
dessert are more obvious. The dates may be replaced with
other dried fruits if you prefer.

¼ cup apple juice
*3 cups peeled and sliced
    dessert apples*
*½ teaspoon ground
    cinnamon*

⅔ cup chopped dates
⅔ cup plain yogurt
¼ cup sour cream
*2 tablespoons slivered
    almonds, toasted*

Serves 4
Preparation time:
10 minutes, plus
cooling
Cooking time:
15–20 minutes
Freezing:
Not recommended

1. Place the apple juice with the apples, cinnamon and
dates in a heavy-based pan, cover and cook gently for
15–20 minutes until softened, stirring occasionally. Leave
to cool.
2. Mix the yogurt and cream together until smooth.
3. Place half of the apple mixture in 4 individual glasses
and cover with half of the yogurt mixture. Repeat the
layers. Chill until required.
4. Sprinkle with the almonds to serve.

PRUNES IN BRANDY

1 cup pitted dried prunes	*2 tablespoons brandy*
1¹/₂ cups orange juice	*2 oranges*

1. Place the prunes and orange juice in a pan and leave to soak for 30 minutes. Bring to the boil, then cover and cook for 20 minutes. Add the brandy and leave to cool.
2. Meanwhile, peel the zest from the oranges and use to make orange rind shreds (see page 8). Peel the pith from the oranges, then cut the flesh into segments, discarding all pith, and add to the prunes.
3. Spoon into individual glass dishes, sprinkle with the orange shreds and chill until required.
4. Serve with Greek yogurt or sour cream if you wish.

Serves 6
Preparation time:
10 minutes, plus
soaking time
Cooking time:
20 minutes
Freezing:
Not recommended

SUMMER SUNDAES

A variation of summer pudding, a popular dessert in England. Ideal to serve at an 'al fresco' meal in the summer.

*4 cups mixed blackberries,
    blueberries and
    redcurrants
2 tablespoons honey*

*2 cups sliced strawberries
    or 1 cup raspberries
8 slices whole wheat bread*

**Serves 8
Preparation time:**
30 minutes, plus
chilling
Cooking time:
10 minutes
Freezing:
Recommended, if
made in freezer-
proof dishes

1. Place the blackberries, blueberries and redcurrants, honey and 2 tablespoons water in a heavy-based pan and cook gently for 10 minutes until tender, stirring occasionally.
2. Add the strawberries or raspberries and leave to cool. Strain, reserving the juice.
3. Cut out 16 circles of bread to fit inside 8 wine glasses and soak in the reserved juice.
4. Place a third of the fruit in the wine glasses and top with a circle of bread. Place another third of the fruit on top and cover with another circle of bread. Top with the remaining fruit. Chill for 30 minutes or until required.
5. Serve with cream or sour cream if you wish.

STAR FRUIT SALAD

Star fruit, sometimes called Carambola, should be yellow-ish when ripe. The fluted edges begin to go brown, so are best trimmed away with scissors. If unavailable, kiwi fruit makes an equally good addition to this fruit salad.

*15 oz can lychees in syrup
juice of 1 lime
2 tablespoons Cointreau
2 oranges*

*1 small Gallia melon,
    halved and seeded
3 star fruit
1/2 tablespoon shredded
    lemon balm*

**Serves 6
Preparation time:**
20 minutes
Freezing:
Not recommended

1. Place the lychees with their syrup, lime juice and Cointreau in a bowl.
2. Peel the oranges and cut into segments, discarding all pith. Cut the melon flesh into cubes or scoop into balls, then add to the bowl with the oranges.
3. Cut the brown ribs from the star fruit, using scissors. Cut the star fruit into slices and add to the bowl.
4. Mix together well, turn into a glass serving dish and sprinkle with the lemon balm. Chill until required.

HOT DESSERTS

STUFFED PEACHES

A well-known Italian recipe which is delicious served
warm, or cold with Melba Sauce*.

*4 large firm peaches,
    halved and pitted
1 cup crushed macaroons
1 egg white*

*2 teaspoons superfine
    sugar
2 tablespoons chopped
    almonds*

Serves 4
Preparation time:
15 minutes
Cooking time:
30 minutes
Freezing:
Not recommended

1. Scoop out a little flesh from the hollows in the peaches
and mash with a fork.
2. Place in a bowl with the macaroon crumbs, egg white
and sugar and mix together.
3. Divide the mixture between the peaches and shape into
mounds. Sprinkle with the almonds.
4. Place in a buttered ovenproof dish and bake in a 350°F
oven for 30 minutes. Serve warm or cold.

CHERRY CLAFOUTIS

A traditional French dessert made with fresh black
cherries. If unobtainable, use a 15 oz can drained black
cherries instead.

*1¼ lb black cherries, pitted
½ cup all-purpose flour,
    sifted
¼ cup superfine sugar*

*3 eggs
1¼ cups milk
¼ teaspoon vanilla*

Serves 6
Preparation time:
15 minutes
Cooking time:
About 35–40
minutes
Freezing:
Not recommended

1. Place the cherries in a single layer in an 8 inch pie plate.
2. Place the flour and sugar in a mixing bowl and make a
well in the center. Add the eggs and half of the milk and
beat together, gradually incorporating all the flour.
3. Add the remaining milk and the vanilla, then pour over
the cherries. Bake in a 375°F oven for about 35–40
minutes, until puffed up and golden brown.
4. Serve with sour cream if you wish.

HOT BLUEBERRY COMPOTE

This very easy and quickly prepared dessert is particularly
luscious with the geranium leaf flavor.

4 cups blueberries
1/4 cup honey
*2 tablespoons freshly
squeezed orange juice*

*2 lemon-scented geranium
leaves (optional)*

Serves 4
Preparation time:
5 minutes
Cooking time:
15 minutes
Freezing:
Recommended

1. Place all the ingredients in a pan and cook very gently
for about 15 minutes, until softened.
2. Remove the geranium leaves, if used. Leave to cool
slightly, then spoon into individual glass dishes. Serve with
cream or sour cream.

DRUNKEN PLUMS

1 lb plums
3 tablespoons honey

3 tablespoons port

Serves 4
Preparation time:
10 minutes
Cooking time:
30–40 minutes
Freezing:
Recommended

1. Make a slit in the side of each plum along the natural
division of the fruit.
2. Place in an ovenproof dish and drizzle over the honey.
Pour over the port, cover and cook in a 325°F oven for
30–40 minutes, depending on the ripeness of the fruit.
3. Serve with whipped cream or sour cream.

SUMMER FRUIT GRATIN

*1/2 small pineapple, peeled
and cored*
1 cup strawberries, halved
*2 nectarines, halved, pitted
and sliced*

*2 kiwi fruit, peeled and
sliced*
1 cup heavy cream
*2 tablespoons superfine
sugar*

Serves 4
Preparation time:
10 minutes
Cooking time:
2–3 minutes
Freezing:
Not recommended

1. Cut the pineapple into thin slices, then halve the slices.
2. Arrange attractively on individual heatproof plates with
the other fruits.
3. Pour over the cream and sprinkle with the sugar.
4. Broil for 2–3 minutes, until beginning to caramelize.
Serve immediately.

FRUIT KEBABS

A very quick dessert, but most attractive to serve. Especially delicious if served flambéd, but also good with Mango Sauce*.

½ pineapple
12 strawberries
½ × 15 oz can lychees in syrup, drained
¼ lb black grapes, seeded

2 tablespoons superfine sugar
3 tablespoons brandy
strawberry leaves to decorate

Serves 6
Preparation time:
15 minutes
Cooking time:
1 minute
Freezing:
Not recommended

1. Peel the pineapple, remove and discard the central hard core, then cut the flesh into chunks.
2. Thread all of the fruit, alternately, onto 12 wooden skewers. Sprinkle with the sugar.
3. Broil for about 1 minute until heated; do not overcook. Arrange on a heatproof dish.
4. Warm the brandy in a ladle or small saucepan, ignite and pour over the fruit. Decorate with strawberry leaves and serve immediately.

HUNZA APRICOT COMPOTE

These tiny little apricots grow wild in the Hunza Valley of Northern India. They are a rather dull brown color because they have been dried naturally—not treated to preserve their color, as is the usual practice with dried apricots. They are extremely sweet and therefore need no added sugar.

½ lb Hunza apricots
⅔ cup orange juice
1¼ cups water
8 kumquats, sliced thinly

2 tablespoons toasted slivered almonds (optional)

Serves 4
Preparation time:
10 minutes, plus soaking time
Cooking time:
15 minutes
Freezing:
Not recommended

1. Soak the apricots in the orange juice and water for 2 hours.
2. Bring to the boil, then simmer gently for 10 minutes. Add the kumquats and simmer for 5 minutes.
3. Turn into a serving bowl and sprinkle with the almonds if using. Serve with sour cream, yogurt or whipped cream.

BLUEBERRY CRUMBLE

4 cups blueberries
3 tablespoons honey
1 1/2 cups whole wheat flour
1/3 cup margarine

1/4 cup dark brown sugar,
*   packed*
1/2 cup chopped filberts

1. Place the blueberries in a 1 quart ovenproof dish and drizzle over the honey.
2. Place the flour in a bowl and rub in the margarine until the mixture resembles breadcrumbs. Stir in the sugar and hazelnuts, then sprinkle over the fruit.
3. Bake in a 400°F oven for 25–30 minutes, until golden. Serve with sour cream, yogurt or whipping cream.

Serves 4
Preparation time:
15 minutes
Cooking time:
25–30 minutes
Freezing:
Recommended

CREPES WITH PETITS SUISSES CHEESE

FOR THE BATTER:
1 cup whole wheat flour
1 teaspoon ground
   cinnamon
1¼ cups milk
1 egg
1 tablespoon salad oil
FOR THE FILLING:
1 orange

12 Petits Suisses or 1½ cups
   cream cheese whipped
   with ⅓ cup lemon juice
1 tablespoon honey
TO FINISH:
2 tablespoons butter, melted
powdered sugar to sprinkle
3 tablespoons Grand
   Marnier
orange slices to decorate

Serves 6
Preparation time:
25 minutes, plus
standing time for
batter
Cooking time:
8–10 minutes
Freezing:
Recommended for
pancakes only

1. Place the batter ingredients in a food processor or blender and work until smooth. Pour into a pitcher and leave to stand for 30 minutes.
2. Heat a 6 inch omelet pan and add a few drops of oil. Pour in 1 tablespoon of the batter and tilt the pan to coat the bottom evenly. Cook until the underside is brown, then turn over and cook for 10 seconds. Turn onto a plate.
3. Repeat with the remaining batter, turning each crepe out onto the plate and separating with waxed paper, to make 12 crepes.
4. Grate the rind from the orange, then peel and divide into segments, discarding all pith.
5. Place the Petits Suisses or cream cheese mixture in a bowl, add the honey and orange rind and mix well.
6. Spoon a tablespoon of the mixture onto each crepe and place 1 or 2 orange segments on top. Fold into quarters to make a triangle, enclosing the filling.
7. Place on a greased baking sheet, brush with the butter and sprinkle with powdered sugar. Bake in a 400°F oven for 8–10 minutes.
8. Sprinkle the liqueur over the crepes. Decorate with orange slices and serve immediately, on warmed plates.

HOT APPLE TARTLETS

Attractive individual apple tarts to serve with whipped cream or sour cream on cooler summer days.

12 oz package frozen puff
   pastry, thawed
1½ lb dessert apples,
   peeled, quartered and
   cored

2 tablespoons superfine
   sugar
pinch of grated nutmeg
   (optional)
¼ cups Calvados or
   brandy

1. Roll out the pastry thinly on a floured surface to a ¼ inch thickness and cut out four 6 inch circles. Place on a baking sheet and chill for 20 minutes.

2. Slice the apples thinly and arrange overlapping in concentric circles over the pastry rounds. Sprinkle with the sugar and a little nutmeg if wished.

3. Bake in a 425°F oven for 15–20 minutes, until the apples are tinged brown. Place on individual plates.

4. Heat the Calvados or brandy in a ladle or small pan, then ignite. Pour the flaming liquid over the tarts and serve immediately.

Serves 4
Preparation time: 30 minutes, plus chilling pastry
Cooking time: 15–20 minutes
Freezing: Not recommended

CREAMS, MOUSSES & SOUFFLÉS

LEMON SYLLABUB

One of the most refreshing desserts—ideal to serve after a rich main course. It can also be made with oranges for a change.

6 tablespoons white wine	*1 1/4 cups heavy cream*
3 tablespoons honey	*1 egg white*
finely grated rind and juice	*lemon rind shreds (see*
of 1 lemon	*page 8) to decorate*

Serves 4
Preparation time:
15 minutes, plus soaking time and chilling
Freezing:
Not recommended

1. Place the wine, 1 tablespoon of the honey, the lemon rind and juice in a bowl and leave to soak for about 1 hour.
2. Whip the cream until stiff, then gradually beat in the wine mixture.
3. Beat the egg white until stiff, then beat in the remaining honey. Carefully fold into the cream mixture and spoon into 4 glass dishes. Chill for 30 minutes, or until required.
4. Decorate with lemon rind to serve.

PEACH AND MACAROON MOUSSE

Homemade macaroons are best for this dessert, but you can use amaretti biscuits if you wish. Peaches vary in sweetness, so you might find you need a little more or less honey.

4 peaches	*1 cup broken macaroons*
1 tablespoon honey	*2 tablespoons toasted*
2/3 cup heavy cream, lightly	*slivered almonds*
whipped	*(optional)*

Serves 4
Preparation time:
20 minutes
Freezing:
Not recommended

1. Cut 12 thin slices from 1 peach and set aside for decoration. Peel and chop the remaining peaches.
2. Place half of the chopped peaches and the honey in a blender or food processor and work until smooth.
3. Fold into the cream with the macaroons and remaining chopped peaches.
4. Spoon into 4 glass dishes and sprinkle with the almonds if using. Decorate with the reserved peach slices.

MANGO AND LIME WHIP

I think mangoes are the most delicious of fruits, tasting somewhere between a strong peach and an orange. Their flavor is enhanced by the use of lime.

2 mangoes
3 tablespoons honey
juice of 1 lime

1¹/₄ cups heavy cream,
  whipped
1 egg white

Serves 6
Preparation time:
20 minutes
Freezing:
Recommended

1. Cut the mangoes either side of the pit; remove 3 slices of mango, cut in half and set aside for decoration. Scoop out all the flesh and place in a blender or food processor. Add the honey and lime juice and work until smooth. Fold into the cream carefully.
2. Beat the egg white until stiff, then fold into the mango cream.
3. Spoon into glass serving dishes and decorate with the reserved mango slices.

CRUNCHY GOOSEBERRY WHIP

This dessert looks very attractive served in tall glasses.

1 lb gooseberries
3 tablespoons honey
1¹/₄ cups heavy cream,
  whipped
3 tablespoons butter or
  margarine

1¹/₂ cups whole wheat
  breadcrumbs
¹/₄ cup chopped filberts,
  toasted
2 tablespoons light brown
  sugar

Serves 4
Preparation time:
20 minutes
Cooking time:
15 minutes
Freezing:
Not recommended

1. Place the gooseberries in a pan with 1 tablespoon water, cover and cook gently for 15 minutes, until soft.
2. Cool slightly, then puree in a blender or food processor; sieve to remove the tops and tails. Add the honey and leave to cool, then stir in the whipped cream.
3. Melt the butter or margarine in a frying pan, add the breadcrumbs and fry until golden brown. Leave to cool, then stir in the filberts and sugar.
4. Divide half of the gooseberry whip between 4 glasses and cover with half of the crumbs. Repeat the layers, finishing with crumbs.

JUNKET

Once a popular dessert in Britain, but one seldom seen nowadays. Very simple to make and delicious served with red fruit compotes or simply with cream.

2½ cups milk
1 tablespoon superfine sugar

1 teaspoon rennet
1 tablespoon rosewater
grated nutmeg to finish

1. Place the milk and sugar in a heavy-based pan and heat gently, stirring until the sugar has dissolved.
2. Cool the milk to lukewarm, then stir in the rennet and rosewater.
3. Pour into a shallow bowl or individual dishes, cover with muslin or foil and leave to stand at room temperature for 15 minutes, or until set.
4. Sprinkle with nutmeg and chill before serving.

Serves 4
Preparation time: 5 minutes, plus setting and chilling time
Freezing: Not recommended

ST CLEMENTS SOUFFLÉ

3 eggs, separated
½ cup superfine sugar
grated rind and juice of
*   1 orange and 1 lemon*
1 envelope gelatin, soaked
*   in 3 tablespoons cold*
*   water*
1¼ cups heavy cream,
*   whipped*

TO FINISH:
½ cup finely chopped
*   almonds, toasted*
6 tablespoons heavy cream,
*   whipped*
lemon rind shreds (see
*   page 8)*

Serves 6–8
Preparation time:
45 minutes, plus
setting time
Freezing:
Recommended

1. Tie a double band of foil around the outside of a 6 inch
soufflé dish, to stand 2 inches above rim.
2. Place the egg yolks, sugar, and orange and lemon rinds
in a bowl. Heat the orange and lemon juice in a small pan
until warm, then pour over the egg mixture. Beat, using an
electric beater, until thick and mousse-like.
3. Heat the gelatin gently until dissolved, then add to the
mixture with the cream, folding in carefully.
4. Beat the egg whites until fairly stiff. Fold 1 tablespoon
into the mixture to lighten, then fold in the rest.
5. Turn into the prepared soufflé dish and chill for about
2 hours, until set.
6. Remove the foil carefully, using a hot knife if necessary.
Press the chopped almonds around the side. Decorate the
top with piped cream and lemon rind shreds.

GOOSEBERRY ELDERFLOWER FOOL

Pick the elderflowers when they are newly in flower.

1 lb gooseberries
½ cup superfine sugar
3 heads elderflower
⅔ cup sour cream

⅔ cup heavy cream,
*   whipped*
frosted leaves (see page 42)
*   to decorate*

Serves 6
Preparation time:
15 minutes
Cooking time:
15 minutes
Freezing:
Recommended

1. Place the gooseberries, sugar, and the elderflower
heads tied in muslin in a pan, cover and cook gently for
about 15 minutes, until soft.
2. Remove the elderflower heads. Leave the fruit to cool
slightly, then puree in a blender or food processor.
3. Fold the sour cream into the cream, then fold into the
gooseberry puree. Divide between 6 dishes, decorate with
frosted leaves and serve with crisp cookies.

RASPBERRY FOOL AND STRAWBERRIES

4 cups halved strawberries
1 cup raspberries
3 tablespoons powdered
   sugar, sifted

1¹/₄ cups heavy cream,
   whipped
strawberry leaves to
   decorate

Serves 6
Preparation time:
15 minutes, plus
chilling
Freezing:
Not recommended

1. Place the strawberries in 6 individual dishes.
2. Rub the raspberries through a nylon sieve, then mix in the powdered sugar. Beat into the cream, then spoon over the strawberries. Chill for at least 20 minutes, then serve, decorated with strawberry leaves.

BLUEBERRY SOUFFLÉ

If you really want to emphasize the blueberry flavor, whip the cream with 2 tablespoons creme de cassis.

3 cups blueberries
1 tablespoon honey
3 eggs, separated
¹/₃ cup superfine sugar
1 envelop gelatin, soaked
   in 3 tablespoons cold
   water
1¹/₄ cups heavy cream,
   whipped

TO FINISH:
¹/₂ cup finely chopped
   almonds, toasted
¹/₃ cup heavy cream,
   whipped
frosted leaves (see page 42)

Serves 8
Preparation time:
45 minutes, plus
setting time
Cooking time:
About 10 minutes
Freezing:
Recommended

1. Tie a double band of foil around the outside of a 6 inch soufflé dish, to stand 2 inches above rim.
2. Place the blueberries in a pan with the honey and 2 tablespoons water, cover and simmer for about 10 minutes, until softened. Leave to cool, then puree in a blender or food processor; sieve to remove the seeds.
3. Place the egg yolks and superfine sugar in a bowl and beat with an electric beater until thick and mousse-like.
4. Heat the gelatin gently until dissolved, then add to the blueberry puree. Fold into the mousse with the cream.
5. Beat the egg whites until fairly stiff. Fold 1 tablespoon into the mixture to lighten, then fold in the rest.
6. Turn into the prepared soufflé dish and chill for about 2 hours, until set.
7. Remove the foil carefully, using a hot knife if necessary. Press the chopped almonds around the side. Decorate the top with piped cream and frosted leaves.

RASPBERRY TANSY

Tansies were popular in 17th-century Britain. They took their name from the pungent herb which originally flavored them. They were made with custard, but using cream cheese is much faster.

1 cup raspberries
1 cup cream cheese
*   whipped with 1/3 cup*
*   lemon juice*

3 tablespoons honey
2/3 cup heavy cream,
*   whipped*

1. Sieve the raspberries; reserve 3 tablespoons of the puree and gradually mix the rest with the cream cheese and honey, until smooth.
2. Fold in the cream, then divide between 6 glass dishes.
3. Lightly fold a dessertspoonful of the reserved puree into each dessert, to give a marbled effect.

Serves 6
Preparation time:
15 minutes
Freezing:
Not recommended

CHEESE & YOGURT DESSERTS

BLACKBERRY BRULEES

Any red fruit can be used instead of blackberries.

1 cup cream cheese
¼ cup plain yogurt
1 tablespoon rosewater
2 teaspoons honey
1 cup blackberries

3 tablespoons chopped almonds
2 tablespoons light brown sugar

Serves 4
Preparation time:
15 minutes, plus chilling
Freezing:
Not recommended

1. Place the cream cheese, yogurt, rosewater and honey in a bowl and mix together until smooth.
2. Divide the blackberries between 4 ramekins and cover with the cheese mixture, smoothing the tops.
3. Mix the almonds with the sugar and sprinkle over the top of each ramekin to cover completely.
4. Broil for 2–3 minutes, until the sugar caramelizes. Chill for 30 minutes before serving.

RASPBERRY GLORY

Make this healthy dessert with any soft fruit of your choice.

½ lb raspberries
1 cup curd cheese or farmer's cheese
1 tablespoon honey

1¼ cups sour cream or Greek yogurt
2 tablespoons chopped almonds, toasted

Serves 4
Preparation time:
15 minutes
Freezing:
Not recommended

1. Rub half of the raspberries through a sieve to make a puree. Gradually add the curd cheese or farmer's cheese and honey and mix until smooth.
2. Divide a third of the whole raspberries between 4 tall glasses, then add a spoonful of the raspberry cheese to each.
3. Stir the sour cream or yogurt until smooth, then spoon half over the cheese mixture. Repeat the layers. Arrange the remaining raspberries on top and spoon over the rest of the raspberry cheese.
4. Decorate with the chopped almonds to serve.

RASPBERRY CHEESECAKE

2 tablespoons butter,
  melted
2 cups crushed graham
  crackers
2 cups raspberries
1¹/₂ cups cream cheese
  whipped with ¹/₃ cup
  lemon juice

2 tablespoons honey
1 tablespoon gelatin,
  soaked in 3 tablespoons
  water
²/₃ cup heavy cream,
  whipped

Serves 8
Preparation time:
30 minutes, plus
setting time
Freezing:
Recommended

1. Combine the butter and graham cracker crumbs. Press over the base of an 8 inch springform pan. Chill until firm.
2. Meanwhile, rub the raspberries through a nylon sieve.
3. Place the cream cheese mixture and honey in a bowl, blend well, then stir in all but 2 tablespoons of the raspberry puree.
4. Heat the gelatin gently until dissolved, then stir into the raspberry mixture.
5. Fold in the cream, then spoon over the crumb base, smoothing the surface. Spoon the remaining puree into a waxed paper piping bag and pipe a series of circles on top. Use a skewer to swirl the puree into a pattern.
6. Chill in the refrigerator for about 1 hour, until set. Remove from the pan and place on a plate to serve.

STRAWBERRY CHEESE PUFFS

8 oz package puff pastry
beaten egg to glaze
2 tablespoons chopped
  almonds

FOR THE FILLING:
²/₃ cup cream chesse
  whipped with 3 table-
  spoons lemon juice
1 teaspoon honey
1 cup sliced strawberries

Makes 5 puffs
Preparation time:
15 minutes, plus
chilling
Cooking time:
8–10 minutes
Freezing:
Not recommended

1. Roll the pastry out very thinly on a floured surface into a rectangle measuring 10 × 15 inches. Cut in half lengthways, then cut into ten 3 inch wide rectangles. Place well apart on baking sheets and chill for 15 minutes.
2. Brush half of the pastry rectangles with beaten egg and sprinkle with the almonds. Bake all of the rectangles in a 425°F oven for 8–10 minutes, until golden brown and crisp right through. Cool on a rack.
3. Mix the cream cheese mixture and honey together and place a spoonful on each plain pastry rectangle. Arrange some strawberries on top, then cover with the nutty rectangles.

APPLE AND BLACKBERRY CHEESE

I like to use Granny Smiths or Golden Delicious for their
flavor in this recipe.

$2^1/2$ cups peeled, cored and
 sliced dessert apples
$1^1/2$ cups blackberries
1 tablespoon honey

1 cup cream cheese
frosted leaves (see page 42)
 to decorate

1. Place the apples, blackberries and honey in a heavy-
based pan, cover and simmer for 15 minutes, until soft.
2. Cool slightly, then place in a blender or food processor
and work until smooth. Sieve to remove seeds.
3. Place the cream cheese in a bowl and gradually mix in
the fruit puree, until blended.
4. Spoon into 4 dishes and decorate with frosted leaves.

Serves 4
Preparation time:
15 minutes
Cooking time:
15 minutes
Freezing:
Recommended

CREME SUCREE

A light, refreshing dessert which can be assembled in minutes. Creme Sucree is equally delicious served with strawberries or other soft fruit.

1¼ cups heavy cream   *2 tablespoons dark brown*
1¼ cups plain yogurt   *sugar*

Serves 4
Preparation time:
10 minutes, plus chilling
Freezing:
Not recommended

1. Whip the cream until it stands in stiff peaks. Fold in the yogurt, then spoon into 4 glass dishes.
2. Sprinkle with the sugar and chill for 1 hour to dissolve the sugar, before serving.

CŒURS A LA CREME

These heart-shaped desserts come from France, where they are served with cream. They are also delicious served with strawberries, but I like them best with Strawberry or Melba Sauce. If you do not have the little heart-shaped molds, you can drain the cheese mixture in a muslin-lined nylon sieve, turn it out whole, and serve it cut into wedges.

1¼ cups cream cheese   *⅔ cup heavy cream,*
whipped with ¼ cup   *whipped*
lemon juice   *⅔ cup Strawberry or*
2 teaspoons honey   *Melba Sauce* to serve*

Serves 4
Preparation time:
25 minutes, plus overnight draining
Freezing:
Not recommended

1. Mix the cream cheese mixture and honey together until smooth, then fold in the cream.
2. Line 4 heart-shaped molds with muslin, spoon in the cheese mixture and smooth the tops. Place on a plate in the refrigerator and leave to drain overnight.
3. Turn the desserts onto individual plates and pour a little strawberry or Melba sauce around each one.

COINTREAU CURD CUPS

1 orange
1 cup curd cheese or
    farmer's cheese
2 tablespoons honey

1 tablespoon Cointreau
$^1/_2$ cup sour cream
1 egg white

Serves 4
Preparation time:
10 minutes, plus
chilling
Freezing:
Not recommended

1. Grate the rind coarsely from a quarter of the orange
and set aside for decoration. Grate the remaining rind
finely.
2. Place the curd cheese in a bowl, then beat in the grated
orange rind, honey and Cointreau.
3. Gradually mix in the sour cream until smooth.
4. Beat the egg white until it forms stiff peaks, then
carefully fold into the cheese mixture.
5. Spoon into 4 glass dishes or ramekins and chill for 15
minutes. Top with the orange shreds to serve.

LEMON CHEESECAKE

$^1/_4$ cup butter
3 cups crushed graham
    crackers
2 cups curd cheese or
    farmer's cheese
2 tablespoons honey
1$^1/_4$ cups sour cream
3 eggs, separated

grated rind and juice of
    1 large lemon
1 tablespoon gelatin,
    soaked in 3 tablespoons
    water
lemon rind shreds (see
    page 8) to decorate

Serves 8
Preparation time:
35 minutes, plus
setting time
Freezing:
Recommended

1. Melt the butter in a pan, then stir in the graham cracker
crumbs. Press over the base of an 8 inch sprungform pan.
Chill until firm.
2. Meanwhile, place the cheese, honey and sour cream in
a bowl and mix together until smooth. Set aside a quarter
of this mixture for decoration.
3. Add the egg yolks and grated lemon rind and juice to
the remaining mixture and mix well.
4. Heat the gelatin gently until dissolved, then add to the
lemon mixture.
5. Beat the egg whites until stiff, then fold into the mixture. Pour over the crumb base.
6. Chill for about 2 hours, until set.
7. Remove from the pan and place the cheesecake on a
serving plate. Place the reserved cheese mixture in a
piping bag fitted with a fluted nozzle and pipe a border
around the edge. Decorate with lemon shreds.

YOGURT FRUIT SALAD

A quick and easy dessert; use any combination of fruit.

1¼ cups plain yogurt
2 teaspoons honey
1 banana

1½ cups sliced strawberries
*2 tablespoons slivered
    almonds, toasted*

1. Mix the yogurt and honey together until smooth.
2. Slice the banana and fold into the yogurt mixture with the strawberries.
3. Spoon into 4 wine glasses or individual dishes and sprinkle with the almonds to serve.

Serves 4
Preparation time:
10 minutes
Freezing:
Not recommended

SORBETS

MELON WITH RASPBERRY SORBET

If you have time, scoop out the melon flesh with a melon baller and chill in the refrigerator. Serve the scoops of sorbet and melon in the melon shell.

*2 small, very ripe
cantaloupe melons,
chilled
1/2 quantity Raspberry
Sorbet (page 48)*

*2 tablespoons framboise
liqueur or kirsch
frosted raspberry leaves
(see below)*

Serves 4
Preparation time:
10 minutes, plus
making sorbet
Freezing:
Not recommended

1. Cut the melons in half, scoop out and discard the seeds. Cut a thin slice from the base of each half so that they stand firmly.
2. Scoop some raspberry sorbet into each cavity, pour over a little liqueur and decorate with frosted leaves. Serve immediately.

To prepare frosted leaves and fruit: Brush the chosen leaves or fruit with egg white, then dip in superfine sugar to coat. Place on waxed paper and leave for 1–2 hours, until dry. Use to decorate desserts.

KIWI SHERBET

Make sure the fruit is soft so that the fragrance, which only comes with ripeness, has developed.

*3 kiwi fruit, peeled
1 1/2 cups apple juice*

*2 tablespoons honey
1 egg white*

Serves 6
Preparation time:
10 minutes
Freezing time:
About 5 hours

1. Mash the kiwi fruit with a fork to form a puree. Mix with the apple juice and honey, then pour into a rigid freezer-proof container. Cover, seal and freeze for about 3 hours, until slushy. Turn out into a bowl.
2. Beat the egg whites until fairly stiff, then beat into the kiwi ice. Return to the container, cover, seal and freeze for about 2 hours, until firm.
3. Transfer to the refrigerator 20 minutes before serving, to soften. Scoop into chilled glasses to serve.

ROSE HIP SORBET

Any of the perfumed teas may be used for making sorbets—they have beautifully delicate flavors.

3 rose hip tea bags   *juice of ½ lemon*
2 cups boiling water   *1 tablespoon rosewater*
⅓ cup superfine sugar   *1 egg white*

Serves 4
Preparation time:
20 minutes
Freezing time:
About 5 hours

1. Place the tea bags in a pitcher and pour on the boiling water. Add the sugar and set aside for 10 minutes.
2. Remove the tea bags, then add the lemon juice and rosewater and pour into a rigid, freezerproof container. Cover, seal and freeze for about 3 hours, until half-frozen. Turn into a bowl.
3. Beat the egg white until stiff, then beat into the half-frozen sorbet. Return to the container, cover, seal and freeze for about 2 hours, until firm.
4. Transfer to the refrigerator 10 minutes before serving, to soften. Scoop into chilled glasses to serve.

GUAVA SORBET

Canned guavas make a very good sorbet. Their subtle perfumed flavor is enhanced by the passion fruit.

14 oz can guavas in syrup   *2 passion fruit*
⅔ cup orange juice   *1 egg white*
¼ cup powdered sugar

Serves 4
Preparation time:
20 minutes
Freezing time:
About 5 hours

1. Place the guavas and their syrup, orange juice and powdered sugar in a blender or food processor and work until smooth; sieve to remove the seeds.
2. Halve the passion fruit and scoop the flesh into a sieve over a bowl. Press through the sieve to extract as much juice as possible. Stir into the guava puree.
3. Pour into a rigid freezerproof container, cover, seal and freeze for about 3 hours, until slushy. Turn into a bowl.
4. Beat the egg white until stiff, then beat into the half-frozen guava puree. Return to the container, cover, seal and freeze for about 2 hours, until firm.
5. Transfer to the refrigerator 20 minutes before serving, to soften. Scoop into chilled glasses or shape into ovals using 2 spoons, then arrange on 4 chilled plates.

PEAR SORBET

*1½ lb ripe dessert pears,
    peeled, quartered and
    cored*
⅔ cup apple juice
⅓ cup superfine sugar
*Eau de Vie de Poires
    Williams liqueur
    (optional)*

1 egg white
TO SERVE:
*1 dessert pear, cored, sliced
    and sprinkled with
    lemon juice*

Serves 4
Preparation time:
20 minutes
Cooking time:
10–15 minutes
Freezing time:
About 5 hours

1. Place the pears, apple juice and sugar in a pan, cover and simmer gently for 10–15 minutes, until soft. Pour into a food processor or blender and work until smooth.
2. Pour into a rigid freezerproof container and leave to cool. Add the liqueur, if using, then cover, seal and freeze for about 3 hours, until half-frozen. Turn out into a bowl.
3. Beat the egg white until stiff, then beat into the half-frozen pear puree. Return to the container, cover, seal and freeze for about 2 hours, until firm.
4. Transfer to the refrigerator 20 minutes before serving, to soften.
5. Shape the sorbet into ovals, using 2 spoons, and arrange on 4 chilled plates with the pear slices, to serve.

GERANIUM LEAF WATER ICE

The leaves of the sweet-scented geranium give a lovely perfume and flavor to this sorbet. There are many varieties, all with different perfumes.

2 cups water
1/2 cup superfine sugar
thinly pared rind and juice
of 2 lemons

3 sweet-scented geranium
leaves
1 egg white
tiny geranium leaves to
decorate

1. Place the water, sugar, lemon rind and geranium leaves in a pan and heat gently, stirring until the sugar has dissolved. Bring to the boil, then simmer for 5 minutes. Add the lemon juice, cover and leave to cool.
2. Strain into a rigid freezerproof container, cover, seal and freeze for about 3 hours, until half-frozen. Turn into a bowl.
3. Beat the egg white until stiff, then beat into the half-frozen ice. Return to the container, cover, seal and freeze for about 2 hours, until firm.
4. Transfer to the refrigerator 20 minutes before serving, to soften. Scoop into chilled glasses and decorate with geranium leaves to serve.

Serves 6
Preparation time:
20 minutes
Freezing time:
About 5 hours

RASPBERRY SORBET

The flavor of this sorbet is improved if you add 2 tablespoons framboise liqueur with the honey.

2¹/₂ cups raspberries
1¹/₄ cups water
¹/₃ cup honey

1 egg white
raspberry or mint leaves to decorate

Serves 6
Preparation time:
15 minutes
Freezing time:
About 5 hours

1. Puree the raspberries in a blender or food processor. Rub through a nylon sieve to remove the pips.
2. Mix the puree with the water and honey and pour into a rigid freezerproof container. Cover, seal and freeze for about 3 hours, until half-frozen. Turn into a bowl.
3. Beat the egg white until stiff, then beat into the half-frozen raspberry puree. Return to the container, cover, seal and freeze for about 2 hours, until firm.
4. Ten minutes before serving, scoop onto chilled plates, with a melon baller if you have one, and place in the refrigerator to soften. Decorate with raspberry or mint leaves.

ORANGE GRANITA

A very refreshing water ice that originates in Italy. Granitas are less sweet and more crumbly in texture than sorbets; they are ideal to serve after a very rich meal.

¹/₂ cup superfine sugar
2¹/₂ cups water
thinly pared rind and juice
    of 2 oranges

thinly pared rind and juice
    of 1 lemon
2 tablespoons Cointreau
frosted leaves (see page 42)
    to decorate

Serves 4
Preparation time:
20 minutes
Freezing time:
About 6 hours

1. Place the sugar, water, and orange and lemon rinds in a saucepan and heat gently, stirring until the sugar has dissolved, then boil for 5 minutes. Add the fruit juices and leave to cool.
2. Strain into a rigid freezerproof container, cover, seal and freeze for about 3 hours, until half-frozen. Remove from the freezer, beat well, then return to the freezer for a further 3 hours.
3. Leave at room temperature for 15 minutes, then stir until crumbly. Spoon into tall glasses, pour over a little Cointreau and decorate with the frosted leaves.

STRAWBERRY CHOCOLATE BOX

Always an impressive dessert to serve when strawberries are in season. The chocolate squares can be made in advance and stored in an airtight container.

3 eggs
½ cup light brown sugar, packed
¾ cup whole wheat flour
TO FINISH:
4 oz baker's semi-sweet chocolate, melted
3 tablespoons framboise liqueur or Grand Marnier

2 cups strawberries
2 tablespoons powdered sugar
⅔ cup heavy cream
⅔ cup plain yogurt
frosted leaves (see page 42) to decorate

Serves 6
Preparation time:
45 minutes
Cooking time:
30–35 minutes
Freezing:
Not recommended

1. Grease and line an 8 inch square cake pan.
2. Beat the eggs and sugar together using an electric beater for about 10 minutes, until the mixture is very thick and mousse-like.
3. Carefully fold in the flour, then turn into the prepared pan. Bake in a 375°F oven for 30–35 minutes, until the cake springs back when lightly pressed. Cool on a rack.
4. Pour the melted chocolate onto waxed paper and leave until just set. Cut into 2 inch squares, using a sharp knife and ruler.
5. Sprinkle the liqueur over the sponge cake and place on a serving plate. Set aside 4 strawberries for decoration. Slice the remainder, sprinkle with half of the powdered sugar and mix together gently. Spoon on top of the sponge cake.
6. Whip the cream with the remaining sugar until stiff. Mix the yogurt with a fork until smooth, then carefully fold into the cream.
7. Spread some of the cream mixture over the sides of the cake. Cover with the chocolate squares, overlapping slightly.
8. Place the remaining cream mixture in a piping bag fitted with a fluted nozzle and pipe over the fruit. Cut the reserved strawberries in half and arrange on top of the gateau. Decorate with frosted leaves.

STRAWBERRY ROULADE

The light sponge roll is made with ground almonds. Any soft fruit can be used for the filling.

3 eggs
¹/₂ cup superfine sugar
¹/₂ cup all-purpose flour, sifted
¹/₂ cup ground almonds
1 tablespoon hot water

powdered sugar for dredging
FOR THE FILLING:
2 cups strawberries
1¹/₄ cups heavy cream, lightly whipped

Serves 8
Preparation time:
45 minutes
Cooking time:
8–10 minutes
Freezing:
Not recommended

1. Grease and line a 12 × 8 inch jelly roll pan.
2. Beat eggs and sugar together using an electric beater, until very thick and mousse-like. Carefully fold in the flour and almonds, adding the water when almost folded in.
3. Turn the mixture into the prepared pan and bake in a 400°F oven for 8–10 minutes, until the cake springs back when lightly pressed.
4. Wring out a clean dish cloth in hot water and lay it on a work surface. Place a sheet of waxed paper on top and sprinkle it with powdered sugar.
5. Turn the sponge roll out onto the paper and remove the lining paper. Trim off the crisp sides of the cake, then roll up with the paper inside the sponge roll. Place on a rack with the join underneath and leave to cool.
6. Set aside a few strawberries and a quarter of the cream for decoration. Chop the remaining strawberries and fold into the rest of the cream.
7. Unroll the sponge roll and remove the waxed paper. Spread the strawberry cream mixture evenly over the sponge roll and roll up again. Place on a serving dish and pipe the reserved cream along the top. Halve the reserved strawberries and use to decorate the roulade.

ICED MERINGUE GATEAU

4 egg whites
1 cup superfine sugar
1 cup ground almonds
FOR THE FILLING:
1 small pineapple, halved, cored and cut up
2 tablespoons kirsch
1 egg white
2 tablespoons honey

1 cup heavy cream, whipped
TO FINISH:
²/₃ cup heavy cream, whipped
¹/₂ cup slivered almonds, toasted
powdered sugar to sprinkle

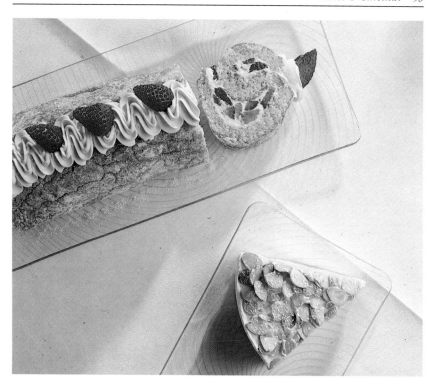

1. Beat the egg whites until stiff and dry, then beat in 4 tablespoons of the sugar. Carefully fold in the remaining sugar and the ground almonds.

2. Put the meringue into a piping bag fitted with a ½ inch plain nozzle and pipe into three 8 inch rounds on baking sheets lined with waxed paper.

3. Bake in a 250°F oven for 2 hours. Cool on the baking sheets, then peel off the paper.

4. To make the filling, put the pineapple in a food processor or blender with the kirsch and work until smooth.

5. Beat the egg white until stiff, then beat in the honey. Fold in the pineapple puree and cream.

6. Trim the meringue rounds to fit inside an 8 inch springform pan and place one meringue round on the base. Spoon over half the pineapple mixture and cover with a second meringue round. Cover with the remaining pineapple mixture and top with the third meringue round. Wrap in a plastic bag, seal and freeze until firm.

7. Remove from the plastic bag and leave to stand at room temperature for 15 minutes. Top with whipped cream and sprinkle with the almonds and powdered sugar to serve. Use a hot knife to cut the gateau cleanly.

Serves 8
Preparation time:
45 minutes
Cooking time:
2 hours
Freezing:
Recommended

STRAWBERRY WALNUT GATEAU

3 eggs
¹/₂ cup light brown sugar,
*   packed*
³/₄ cup whole wheat flour
¹/₂ cup ground walnuts

FOR THE FILLING:
1 ¹/₄ cups heavy cream,
*   whipped*
3¹/₂ cups strawberries,
*   sliced*
¹/₂ cup chopped walnuts

Serves 8
Preparation time:
40 minutes
Cooking time:
20–25 minutes
Freezing:
Not recommended

1. Grease and line a 12 × 8 inch jelly roll pan.
2. Place the eggs and sugar in a bowl and beat with an electric beater for about 10 minutes, until the mixture is very thick and mousse-like.
3. Carefully fold in the flour and ground walnuts.
4. Turn into the prepared pan and bake in a 375°F oven for 20–25 minutes. Turn onto a rack to cool.
5. Set aside a quarter of the cream and a few strawberry slices. Fold the other strawberries and cream together.
6. Cut the cake into 3 equal pieces widthways and sandwich together with a strawberry and cream filling.
7. Spread some of the remaining cream over the sides of the gateau and coat with the chopped walnuts.
8. Spread the rest of the cream over the top of the gateau and decorate with the remaining strawberry slices.

JOHANNISBER KUCHEN

A delicious redcurrant cake which a German friend of mine serves. You can also use apples, plums or pears.

½ cup butter or margarine
½ cup superfine sugar
finely grated rind and juice
of 1 lemon
2 eggs
1½ cups self-rising flour,
sifted

1 tablespoon boiling water
2 cups redcurrants
1 tablespoon powdered
sugar
⅔ cup Redcurrant Sauce*
to serve

1. Grease and line an 8 inch springform pan.
2. Cream the butter or margarine, sugar and lemon rind together until light and fluffy.
3. Beat in the eggs one at a time, adding a tablespoon of flour with the second egg. Fold in the remaining flour with the lemon juice and finally the water.
4. Turn the mixture into the prepared pan. Arrange the redcurrants over the top and sprinkle with the powdered sugar.
5. Bake in a 350°F oven for 50–60 minutes.
6. Leave in the pan for a few minutes, then transfer to a rack to cool. Serve sliced, with the redcurrant sauce.

Serves 6–8
Preparation time:
25 minutes
Cooking time:
50–60 minutes
Freezing:
Not recommended

REDCURRANT MERINGUES

The meringue rounds for these attractive individual desserts can be stored in an airtight container for up to a week.

2 egg whites
¹/₂ cup superfine sugar
FOR THE FILLING:
1 cup redcurrants
1 cup heavy cream

2 tablespoons framboise
liqueur (optional)
2 teaspoons honey
¹/₂ cup raspberries

Serves 8
Preparation time:
35 minutes
Cooking time:
2 hours
Freezing:
Not recommended

1. Beat the egg whites until stiff, then gradually beat in the sugar until the mixture holds its shape.
2. Line 2 baking sheets with waxed paper; draw on eight 3 inch circles and eight 2 inch circles.
3. Put the meringue mixture into a piping bag fitted with a ¹/₂ inch plain nozzle and pipe onto the paper to cover the circles completely.
4. Bake in a 250°F oven for 2 hours. Transfer to a rack to cool.
5. Reserve 8 redcurrants for decoration; strip the rest from their stalks.
6. Whip the cream, liqueur if using, and honey together until thickened, then spoon a quarter of it into a piping bag fitted with a large fluted nozzle.
7. Mix the redcurrants and raspberries into the remaining cream and place a spoonful on each of the large meringue circles. Cover with the small circles.
8. Decorate the top circles with the remaining whipped cream and redcurrants. Serve immediately.

GOOSEBERRY CHARLOTTE

Elderflowers impart a delicate flavor to this delicious charlotte. They are best picked when they begin to flower, early in June, and have a creamy appearance.

1 lb gooseberries
2 heads elderflower
(optional)
2 eggs, plus 1 yolk
¹/₃ cup superfine sugar
1 envelope gelatin, soaked
in 3 tablespoons cold
water

1 cup heavy cream,
whipped
TO FINISH:
30 ladies' fingers
1 kiwi fruit, peeled and
sliced thinly

1. Place the gooseberries in a pan with the elderflower heads tied in muslin if using, and 2 tablespoons water. Cover and cook gently for 10–15 minutes, until soft. Remove the elderflowers and cool slightly.

2. Place in a food processor or blender and work until smooth, then sieve to remove the tops and tails.

3. Place the eggs, egg yolk and sugar in a bowl and beat with an electric beater until thick and mousse-like.

4. Heat the gelatin gently until dissolved, then mix into the gooseberry puree.

5. Set aside 2 tablespoons of the cream. Fold the gooseberry mixture into the rest, then fold into the egg mixture.

6. Turn into a greased 7 inch springform pan and chill for 2 hours, until set.

7. Turn out onto a serving dish, spread the reserved cream round the side and press on the cookies, overlapping them slightly.

8. Decorate the charlotte with the kiwi fruit.

Serves 8
Preparation time: 45 minutes
Setting time: 2 hours
Freezing: Recommended

FRANGIPANE TART

Bing cherries are best for this tart as their sharpness gives
the necessary flavor.

RICH BASIC PASTRY:	FOR THE FILLING:
2 cups all-purpose flour	1 egg
⅔ cup butter or margarine	¼ cup superfine sugar
1 tablespoon superfine	¼ cup soft margarine
sugar	1 cup ground almonds
1 egg yolk	2 drops almond extract
1–2 tablespoons ice water	12 oz can sour cherries in
beaten egg to glaze	syrup, drained

Serves 8
Preparation time:
40 minutes, plus
chilling pastry
Cooking time:
30–35 minutes
Freezing:
Recommended

1. Sift the flour into a bowl and rub in the butter or
margarine until the mixture resembles breadcrumbs. Stir
in the sugar. Add the egg yolk and enough water to mix to a
firm dough. Turn onto a floured surface and knead lightly
until smooth.
2. Cut off two-thirds of the dough, roll out thinly on a
floured surface and use to line an 8 inch pie plate, placed
on a baking sheet. Chill for 30 minutes.
3. Meanwhile, make the filling. Place the egg, sugar,
margarine, ground almonds and almond extract in a bowl
and beat until smooth.
4. Place the cherries in the pie plate and spoon the
almond mixture over the top, levelling the surface with a
palette knife.
5. Roll the remaining pastry out thinly and cut into narrow
strips. Use these to make a lattice pattern over the filling,
moistening the edges of the pastry with water. Brush with
beaten egg.
6. Bake in a 400°F oven for 20 minutes, then lower the
temperature to 375°F and bake for 10–15 minutes, until
firm to the touch and golden. Serve warm or cold.

GOOSEBERRY CREAM TART

A delicious, creamy tart which can also be made with apples or apricots.

PATE SUCREE:
1 1/2 cups all-purpose flour
1/3 cup butter, softened
1/3 cup superfine sugar
3 egg yolks

FOR THE FILLING:
1 lb gooseberries
2 tablespoons superfine
* sugar*
1 cup whipping cream
2 eggs

Serves 8
Preparation time: 30 minutes, plus chilling pastry
Cooking time: 45 minutes
Freezing: Recommended

1. Sift the flour onto a cool work surface, make a well in the center and put in the butter, sugar and egg yolks.
2. Using the fingertips of one hand, work these ingredients together, then draw in the flour and work to a paste. Knead lightly until smooth, wrap in a plastic bag and chill for about 1 hour.
3. Meanwhile prepare the filling. Place the gooseberries, sugar and 2 tablespoons water in a heavy-based pan, cover and cook gently for 10 minutes.
4. Mix together the cream and eggs, then add the gooseberries and mix gently.
5. Turn the dough onto a floured surface, roll out and use to line a 9 inch fluted pie plate, placed on a baking sheet. Chill for 15 minutes.
6. Pour the filling into the pie plate and bake in a 375°F oven for 45 minutes, until golden.
7. Remove the tart carefully from the pie plate. Serve warm or cold.

BLUEBERRY FILO FLOWERS

Filo pastry is now becoming increasingly available in supermarkets. You can make the filo flowers in advance and store them in an airtight container, leaving only the filling to prepare on the day.

1/2 lb filo pastry
2 cups blueberries
2 cups peeled and chopped
* dessert apples*
3 tablespoons honey
1 cup heavy cream,
* whipped*

2 tablespoons apple juice
2 tablespoons creme de
* cassis (optional)*
blueberry or mint leaves to
* decorate*

1. Cut the filo pastry into twenty-four 4 inch squares. Grease the outside of 8 inverted ramekins.

2. Drape 3 squares of filo pastry over each ramekin, so that the corners are separate and resemble flower petals.

3. Place on a baking sheet and bake in a 375°F oven for 6–8 minutes, until golden brown; make sure they do not overcook.

4. Leave to cool, then lift off the ramekin and turn up the right way.

5. Place the blueberries, apples and honey in a pan, cover and bring to the boil, then simmer gently for 10–15 minutes, until softened.

6. Cool slightly, then puree in a food processor or blender. Rub through an nylon sieve and leave until cold.

7. Fold half of the puree into the cream and divide the mixture between the filo flowers.

8. Stir the apple juice and cassis, if using, into the remaining puree and spoon some onto each serving plate to cover the base. Place a filo flower in the center of each plate and decorate each with a leaf.

Serves 8
Preparation time:
40 minutes
Cooking time:
8–10 minutes
Freezing:
Not recommended

STRAWBERRY CREAM TARTLETS

PATE SUCREE:
1 cup all-purpose flour
¼ cup butter, softened
¼ cup superfine sugar
2 egg yolks
FOR THE FILLING:
2 tablespoons whipping
*   cream*

6 Petits Suisses cheeses
1 teaspoon honey
1 cup small strawberries,
*   halved*
FOR THE GLAZE:
¼ cup raspberry jam

Makes 14
Preparation time:
30 minutes, plus
chilling pastry
Cooking time:
10 minutes
Freezing:
Not recommended

1. Make and chill the pate sucree as described on page 60. Roll out thinly on a floured surface and use to line 14 muffin cups. Press a square of foil into each and chill for 15 minutes.
2. Bake 'blind' in a 375°F oven for 10 minutes or until golden brown. Leave to cool, remove the foil and place on a plate.
3. Mix the cream, Petits Suisses and honey together and spoon a little into each tartlet. Top with the strawberries.
4. Heat the raspberry jam until liquid and smooth, then brush generously over the strawberries.

BLACKBERRY SCRUNCH

This can be made with any soft red fruit. It can be prepared in individual ramekins if you prefer.

6 tablespoons salad oil
3 tablespoons honey
2 cups rolled oats
⅓ cup flaked coconut

FOR THE TOPPING:
3 cups blackberries
⅔ cup plain yogurt
1 cup heavy cream,
*   whipped*

Serves 6
Preparation time:
25 minutes
Cooking time:
30–35 minutes
Freezing:
Not recommended

1. Place the oil and honey in a pan and heat gently. Stir in the oats and coconut and mix thoroughly.
2. Sprinkle into a greased 9 inch round pie plate and fork to the edges.
3. Bake in a 350°F oven for 30–35 minutes, until golden. Leave to cool.
4. Sprinkle all but 8 blackberries over the oat mixture. Rub the 8 blackberries through a sieve and set aside.
5. Mix the yogurt until smooth, then fold into the cream. Spoon over the blackberries and smooth to the edges.
6. Drizzle the reserved blackberry puree over the cream and swirl into a pattern with a skewer. Chill until required.

NECTARINE GALETTES

I like to leave the smooth, colorful skin on the nectarines, but they can, of course, be peeled.

¹/₃ cup margarine
¹/₄ cup light brown sugar, packed
1 cup whole wheat flour
³/₄ cup ground filberts, toasted

FOR THE FILLING:
1¹/₄ cups heavy cream
2 tablespoons Grand Marnier
5 nectarines
1 tablespoon lemon juice

Makes 10
Preparation time:
35 minutes
Cooking time:
12–15 minutes
Freezing:
Recommended for pastry only

1. Cream the margarine and sugar together until light and fluffy. Stir in the flour and filberts and mix to a firm dough, using your hand.
2. Turn onto a floured surface and knead lightly until smooth. Roll out the dough thinly and cut out ten 3 inch circles and ten 2 inch circles.
3. Place on a baking sheet and bake in a 350°F oven for 12–15 minutes, until golden. Transfer to a rack to cool.
4. Whip the cream and liqueur together until soft peaks form. Place in a piping bag fitted with a large fluted nozzle.
5. Cut the nectarines into slices and brush with the lemon juice. Arrange half of the nectarine slices on the larger pastry rounds and cover with piped cream whirls. Arrange the remaining nectarine slices on top and cover with the smaller rounds.
6. Decorate with piped cream rosettes.

PASSION FRUIT BASKETS

These pretty little baskets make ideal containers for mousses, whips and ice creams. The mixture makes fourteen so you will be able to freeze some for future use. Do not fill them more than 30 minutes before serving, or they will lose their crispness.

3 tablespoons all-purpose flour, sifted
¹/₃ cup superfine sugar
3 egg whites
2 tablespoons butter or margarine, melted

FOR THE FILLING:
2 passion fruit
2 tablespoons cream cheese
2 tablespoons lemon juice
¹/₃ cup heavy cream
2 teaspoons honey

1. Mix the flour and sugar together in a bowl, add the egg whites and melted fat, and beat together thoroughly until smooth.

2. Place spoonfuls of the mixture well apart on greased and floured baking sheets: spread them thinly to form 5 inch rounds. Bake one batch at a time in a 400°F oven for 4–5 minutes, until golden at the edges.

3. Leave the cookies to cool slightly, then carefully remove each one from the baking sheets with a sharp knife. Place each cookie top side down over the base of an inverted glass. Mold the cookie to give wavy edges, leave to set, then remove carefully.

4. To make the filling, cut the passion fruit in half and scoop out the pulp. Mix with the cream cheese and lemon juice.

5. Whip the cream and honey together, then fold carefully into the cheese mixture. Spoon into the cookie baskets and serve immediately.

Serves 4
Preparation time:
40 minutes
Cooking time:
20 minutes
Freezing:
Recommended for baskets only

FROZEN DESSERTS

MANGO PARFAIT

2 mangoes
juice of 1 lime
½ cup superfine sugar

2 egg whites
1¼ cups heavy cream,
  whipped

Serves 6
Preparation time:
20 minutes
Freezing time:
About 2 hours

1. Cut the mangoes either side of the pit and scoop out all the flesh. Place in a blender or food processor with the lime juice and 1 tablespoon sugar and work to a puree.
2. Transfer to a rigid freezerproof container, cover, seal and freeze for about 2 hours, until half-frozen.
3. Beat the egg whites until stiff, then gradually beat in the remaining sugar.
4. Beat the half-frozen mango puree, then fold into the meringue mixture, with the cream. Spoon into chilled glasses and serve immediately, with crisp cookies.

FROZEN STRAWBERRY BOMBES

8 cups strawberries
1 tablespoon powdered
  sugar
2 tablespoons framboise
  liqueur (optional)
3 egg whites
¾ cup superfine sugar

1¼ cups heavy cream,
  whipped
¼ cup sour cream or
  whipping cream
frosted leaves (see page 42)
  to decorate

Serves 10
Preparation time:
40 minutes
Freezing time:
About 3 hours

1. Puree the strawberries in a blender or food processor, then sieve to remove the pips.
2. Place 1½ cups of the puree in a bowl, stir in the powdered sugar, and liqueur if using, and set aside.
3. Beat the egg whites until stiff, then gradually beat in the superfine sugar until thick. Fold in the heavy cream and remaining strawberry puree.
4. Divide the mixture between ten 1 cup molds, cover with foil and freeze for about 3 hours.
5. To serve, dip the molds into cold water and turn out onto chilled serving plates. Pour a little of the reserved strawberry sauce around each ice.
6. Place the sour cream or whipping cream in a waxed paper piping bag, cut off the end and pipe a design on the sauce. Use a skewer to create a marbled effect. Serve immediately, decorated with frosted leaves.

PLUM ICE CREAM

This looks very pretty served on individual plates, surrounded with the sauce; but if you prefer, serve whole, surrounded with sauce, and slice at the table.

1 lb tart plums
½ cup superfine sugar
2 egg whites
¼ cup powdered sugar, sifted

⅔ cup heavy cream, whipped

Serves 8
Preparation time:
40 minutes
Cooking time:
15 minutes
Freezing time:
About 3 hours

1. Place the plums, superfine sugar and ¼ cup water in a pan, cover and cook gently for 15 minutes, until tender. Cool slightly, remove the pits, then puree in a blender or food processor. Sieve to remove the skins and leave to cool.
2. Beat the egg whites until stiff, then gradually beat in the powdered sugar. Set aside a quarter of the plum puree, then fold the rest into the egg whites with the cream.
3. Turn into a 4½ cup mold or 7½ × 3½ × 2½ inch loaf pan, cover with foil and freeze for about 3 hours, until firm.
4. To serve, dip the pan in cold water and turn out. Cut into slices and place on chilled plates.
5. Pour the reserved plum puree around the ice cream slices to serve.

BLACKBERRY AND GERANIUM BOMBE

Sweet-scented geranium leaves give blackberries a wonderful flavor. Of course you can omit them or add 2 tablespoons rosewater instead. This ice cream also looks attractive made in individual freezerproof molds.

4 cups blackberries
3 sweet-scented geranium leaves
¼ cup superfine sugar
½ cup water
¼ cup sugar
3 egg yolks

2 cups whipping cream, whipped
TO DECORATE:
6 tablespoons whipped cream
8 blackberries
geranium leaves

1. Put the blackberries, geranium leaves and superfine sugar in a pan and simmer for about 10 minutes, until tender. Rub through a sieve and leave to cool.

2. Place the water and ¼ cup sugar in a pan and heat gently, stirring until dissolved. Increase the heat and boil steadily until the syrup reaches 225°F on a candy thermometer, or a little of the cooled syrup forms a thread when drawn between thumb and forefinger.

3. Cool slightly, then pour onto the egg yolks, beating until the mixture is thick and mousse-like.

4. Mix the cream and blackberry puree together, then fold in the egg mixture.

5. Turn into a 6 cup bowl and smooth the surface. Cover with foil and freeze for about 5 hours, until firm.

6. To serve, invert the bowl onto a serving plate and cover with a cloth wrung out in hot water; give a good shake and the ice cream will come out.

7. Pipe a border of cream around the bottom and leave in the refrigerator for about 30 minutes. Just before serving, decorate with the blackberries and geranium leaves.

Serves 8
Preparation time:
45 minutes
Cooking time:
10 minutes
Freezing time:
About 5 hours

LIME ICE CREAM

A refreshing yet very creamy ice cream with a really soft texture, so there is no need to soften before serving.

3 eggs, separated
²/₃ cup superfine sugar
grated rind and juice of
*   2 limes*

1¼ cups heavy cream,
*   whipped*
lime slices to decorate

Serves 8
Preparation time:
20 minutes
Freezing time:
About 3 hours

1. Beat the egg yolks, half of the sugar and the lime rind together until thick and creamy.
2. Strain the lime juice into a pan, heat gently, then pour onto the egg mixture, beating until thick.
3. Beat the egg whites until stiff, then beat in the remaining sugar. Fold in the lime mixture, with the cream.
4. Turn into a rigid freezerproof container, cover, seal and freeze for about 3 hours, until firm.
5. Scoop into chilled glass dishes and decorate with lime slices to serve.

RASPBERRY CREAM BOMBE

2 eggs, plus 2 yolks
¹/₃ cup superfine sugar
2 cups whipping cream
¹/₄ teaspoon vanilla

1¼ cups heavy cream,
*   whipped*
¹/₂ quantity Raspberry
*   Sorbet (page 48),*
*   softened*

Serves 8–10
Preparation time:
40 minutes
Freezing time:
About 3½ hours

1. Mix the eggs, egg yolks and sugar together in a bowl.
2. Bring the whipping cream to the boil, then pour onto the egg mixture, stirring vigorously. Strain, then leave to cool.
3. Add the vanilla and fold in the whipped cream.
4. Pour into a rigid freezerproof container, cover, seal and freeze for about 2 hours, until half-frozen. Beat with an electric beater, cover and return to the freezer for about 30 minutes, until fairly firm.
5. Beat the ice cream to an even consistency, then use to line thickly the inside of a chilled 6 cup bombe mold or bowl.
6. Fill the center with the raspberry sorbet and cover with any remaining ice cream. Put the lid of the bombe mold on, or cover the bowl with foil, and freeze for about 1 hour, until firm.
7. To serve, dip the mold or bowl into cold water and turn the bombe out onto a chilled serving dish.

KULFI

This is an adaptation of a popular ice cream from India. In India it is made entirely with milk, which is boiled long enough to reduce the original quantity by a third. Adding the milk powder gives the same result, but takes less time.

2¹/₂ cups milk
¹/₄ cup skimmed milk
*   powder*
seeds from 4 cardamom
*   pods*

¹/₄ cup superfine sugar
¹/₄ cup finely chopped
*   almonds*
¹/₄ cup finely chopped
*   pistachio nuts*

Serves 4
Preparation time:
20 minutes
Freezing time:
About 4 hours

1. Beat the milk and milk powder together, add the cardamom seeds and bring to the boil. Stir in the sugar, then leave until cold.
2. Strain the milk into a rigid freezerproof container, then stir in the almonds and all but 1 tablespoon of the pistachios. Cover, seal and freeze for about 2 hours, until half-frozen.
3. Beat with an electric beater, cover, seal and return to the freezer for about 2 hours until firm.
4. Transfer to the refrigerator 30 minutes before serving, to soften. Scoop into chilled glasses and sprinkle with the remaining pistachio nuts to serve.

FROZEN CHERRY ROULADE

A roulade is always a spectacular and popular dessert. Here I have added cherries to the filling. As the recipe is served frozen, it can be prepared well in advance of your dinner party.

5 oz baker's semi-sweet
*   chocolate, broken into*
*   pieces*
4 eggs, separated
²/₃ cup superfine sugar
powdered sugar for
*   sprinkling*
FOR THE FILLING:
1 egg white

¹/₄ cup powdered sugar,
*   sifted*
²/₃ cup heavy cream,
*   whipped*
15 oz can black cherries,
*   drained, pitted and*
*   chopped*

1. Grease and line a 12 × 8 inch jelly roll pan.
2. Place the chocolate and 3 tablespoons water in a pan and heat gently until melted.

3. Beat the egg yolks with half of the superfine sugar until thick and creamy, then beat in the warm chocolate.
4. Beat the egg whites until stiff, then beat in the remaining sugar. Fold into the chocolate mixture.
5. Turn into the prepared pan. Bake in a 350°F oven for 30–35 minutes, until firm.
6. Leave to cool for 5 minutes, then cover with a clean damp cloth and leave to stand for 3 hours or overnight.
7. To make the filling, beat the egg white until stiff, then beat in the powdered sugar. Fold in the cream and cherries.
8. Carefully remove the cloth from the roulade and turn out onto a sheet of waxed paper sprinkled thickly with powdered sugar. Peel off the lining paper.
9. Spread the filling over the roulade and roll up like a jelly roll. Freeze uncovered for about 3 hours, until firm, then wrap in a plastic bag until required.
10. Sprinkle with powdered sugar and slice to serve.

Serves 8
Preparation time:
40 minutes, plus standing time
Cooking time:
30–35 minutes
Freezing time:
About 3 hours

PINEAPPLE SLICE

1 large pineapple
3 egg whites
3/4 cup superfine sugar

1 1/4 cups heavy cream,
whipped

Serves 8
Preparation time:
30 minutes
Freezing time:
About 3 hours

1. Cut the pineapple in half lengthways. Scrape out the flesh and juice, using a fork to loosen the flesh and a spoon to scrape the shells clean. Discard the hard central core and chill the shells. Place the flesh in a blender or food processor and work until smooth.
2. Beat the egg whites until stiff, then gradually beat in the sugar. Fold in the cream and pineapple puree.
3. Spoon enough of the mixture into the shells to come to the top and smooth evenly. Cover with foil and freeze for about 3 hours, until firm. Place the remaining mixture in a rigid container, cover, seal and freeze.
4. To serve, cut each pineapple half into 4 slices and place on chilled individual plates. Scoop the remaining ice cream into balls and arrange next to each slice.

COCONUT CREAM ICE

1/2 cup unsweetened flaked
coconut, blended with 3
tablespoons boiling
water
2 eggs, separated
1/2 cup superfine sugar

1 1/4 cups whipping cream
2/3 cup heavy cream,
whipped
2/3 cup Chocolate Sauce*
1/4 cup sour cream or
whipping cream

Serves 8
Preparation time:
20 minutes
Freezing time:
About 3 hours

1. Place the blended coconut, egg yolks and half of the sugar in a bowl and beat well.
2. Bring the whipping cream to the boil, then pour onto the egg mixture, stirring vigorously. Return to the pan and cook gently until thickened slightly. Leave to cool.
3. Beat the egg whites until stiff, then beat in the remaining sugar. Fold in the cream and coconut custard.
4. Turn into a rigid freezerproof container, cover, seal and freeze for about 3 hours, until firm.
5. Transfer to the refrigerator 20 minutes before serving, to soften. Scoop onto individual serving plates and pour round the chocolate sauce.
6. Fill a waxed paper piping bag with the sour cream or whipping cream, cut off the end and pipe a design on the sauce.

FROZEN PASSION FRUIT SOUFFLÉS

Serve as soon as you have removed the foil, or the raised
ice cream will begin to drip.

8 ripe passion fruit
1 teaspoon lemon juice
2 eggs, separated
1/2 cup superfine sugar

1 1/4 cups heavy cream,
 whipped
1/2 cup chopped pistachio
 nuts

Serves 6
Preparation time:
35 minutes
Freezing time:
About 3 hours

1. Tie double bands of foil around the outside of 6 small
freezerproof ramekins, to stand 1 inch above the rims.
2. Cut the passion fruit in half and scoop the pulp into a
sieve over a bowl. Press through the sieve to extract as
much juice as possible; discard the seeds. Stir in the lemon
juice.
3. Place the egg yolks and half of the sugar in a bowl and
beat with an electric beater until thick and mousse-like.
4. Beat the egg whites until stiff then beat in the remaining
sugar. Fold into the egg yolk mixture with the passion fruit
juice and the cream.
5. Spoon into the prepared ramekins, place on a baking
sheet and freeze uncovered for about 3 hours, until firm.
6. Remove the foil carefully and sprinkle the pistachio
nuts over each soufflé to serve.

FROZEN RASPBERRY SPONGE

A cinnamon-flavored sponge cake that encloses a frozen
raspberry filling. Melba sauce completes this simple yet
impressive dessert.

2 eggs
1/3 cup superfine sugar
1/2 cup all-purpose flour
1 teaspoon ground
 cinnamon
FOR THE FILLING:
1 cup raspberries
2 egg whites

1/2 cup superfine sugar
2/3 cup heavy cream,
 whipped
TO FINISH:
2/3 cup Melba Sauce*
frosted raspberry leaves
 (see page 42)

1. Grease and line a 7 inch square cake pan.
2. Place the eggs and sugar in a bowl and beat with an
electric beater, until thick and mousse-like.

3. Sift the flour and cinnamon together, then carefully fold into the beaten mixture.

4. Turn into the prepared pan and bake in a 375°F oven for 25–30 minutes, until the cake springs back when lightly pressed. Cool on a rack.

5. To make the filling, rub the raspberries through a nylon sieve to remove the pips.

6. Beat the egg whites until stiff peaks form, then gradually beat in the sugar. Fold in the raspberry puree and the cream.

7. Split the cake in half horizontally. Place the bottom half in the cleaned cake pan. Spoon the filling over the top, spreading evenly to the edges. Cover with the remaining sponge cake, pressing gently together. Cover with foil and freeze for about 3 hours, until firm.

8. To serve, dip the pan in cold water to loosen the cake and turn out. Cut in half lengthways, then into slices. Place on chilled plates, pour over the melba sauce and decorate with the frosted leaves.

Serves 8
Preparation time:
45 minutes
Cooking time:
25–30 minutes
Freezing time:
About 3 hours

SAUCES

CHOCOLATE SAUCE

Serve with vanilla, chocolate or coffee ice cream.

6 oz baker's semi-sweet chocolate broken into pieces
²/₃ cup water

1 teaspoon instant coffee granules
¹/₄ cup dark brown sugar, packed

Makes 1¹/₄ cups
Preparation time:
8 minutes
Freezing:
Recommended

1. Place all the ingredients in a small pan and heat gently until melted.
2. Stir thoroughly, then simmer gently for about 3 minutes. Serve warm or cold.

MELBA SAUCE

Serve with raspberry or vanilla ice cream.

1³/₄ cups raspberries   *¹/₄ cup honey*

Makes 1 cup
Preparation time:
10 minutes
Freezing:
Recommended

Place the raspberries and honey in a blender or food processor and work until smooth. Rub through a nylon sieve to remove the seeds.

STRAWBERRY SAUCE

Serve with strawberry or vanilla ice cream.

2 cups strawberries
1 tablespoon powdered sugar, sifted

2 tablespoons framboise liqueur or Cointreau

Makes ²/₃ cup
Preparation time:
10 minutes
Freezing:
Recommended

1. Place the strawberries and powdered sugar in a food processor or blender and work until smooth. Rub through a nylon sieve to remove the seeds.
2. Stir in the liqueur.

MANGO SAUCE

For a special dessert, add 2 tablespoons Cointreau or other orange-flavored liqueur. This sauce is delicious with vanilla ice cream.

1 mango　　　　　*²/₃ cup orange juice*

1. Cut the mango either side of the pit and scoop out all the flesh, discarding the pit.
2. Place the flesh in a food processor or blender with the orange juice and work until smooth.
3. Serve warm or cold.

Makes about 1¼ cups
Preparation time: 10 minutes
Freezing: Recommended

CREMETS

Serve with fresh fruit or fruit compotes.

6 tablespoons heavy cream, whipped
¼ cup cream cheese whipped with 2 tablespoons lemon juice

2 teaspoons honey (optional)

Fold the cream into the cream cheese mixture, sweetening with the honey if you wish. Turn into a shallow dish and chill until required.

Makes 1 cup
Preparation time: 10 minutes
Freezing: Recommended

REDCURRANT SAUCE

A fresh, sharp-tasting sauce, ideal to serve with rich, creamy or cake-based desserts.

1½ cups redcurrants　　　*1 tablespoon honey*

1. Rub two-thirds of the redcurrants through a nylon sieve into a bowl.
2. Stir the honey into the redcurrant puree, then stir in the remaining redcurrants.

Makes ²/₃ cup
Preparation time: 10 minutes
Freezing: Recommended

INDEX

Photography by: Charlie Stebbings
Designed by: Sue Storey
Home economist: Carole Handslip
Stylist: Antonia Gaunt
Illustration by: Linda Smith
U.S. Consultant Editor: Carla Capalbo.